Edwina the Cutest Sheep in the World

by Marty Scanlon

illustrated by Penny Weber

This book is dedicated to an angel that came to earth.
She had red hair, a warm smile, and a great laugh.
Her name was Josephine Elmena Gardiner
and she was my Mother.

Edwina Wooley is my name,
and I'm a Blacknose sheep living
at Gardiner's Grange in Virginia.

We have a country home with a large farmhouse and buildings, and lots of Blacknose sheep. Everyone thinks we are the cutest sheep in the world.

In the past my family have lived in
the mountains of Valais, Switzerland.
Now, my family have moved to
different countries.

My Father and Mother are Edwin and Elmena Wooley and they told me that they are making plans to move to Virginia, and reunite our family.

My sisters are Shearly who lives in Scotland,

and Winnie who lives in Wales.

My brother, Ewen, still lives in Switzerland with my parents.

The people I live with at Gardiner's Grange are very nice,

and I really like playing with
their children.

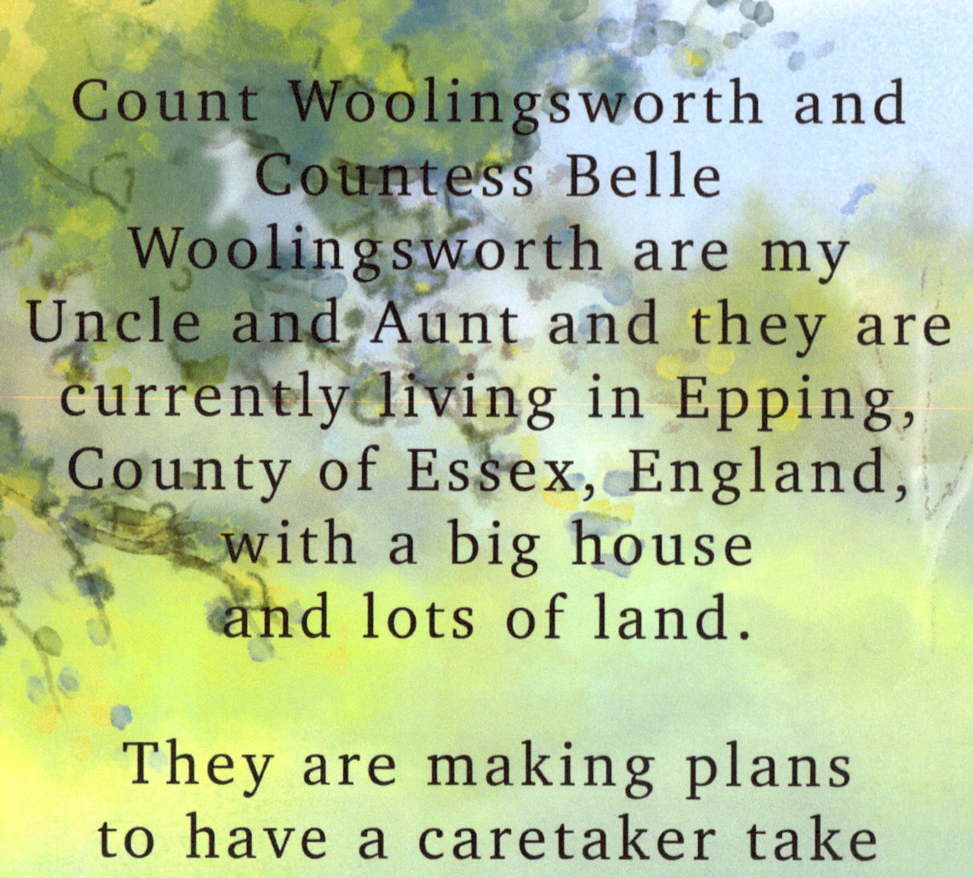

Count Woolingsworth and
Countess Belle
Woolingsworth are my
Uncle and Aunt and they are
currently living in Epping,
County of Essex, England,
with a big house
and lots of land.

They are making plans
to have a caretaker take
care of their land
and travel to
Gardiner's Grange.

My Great Aunt Frances Fleece
lives in France in a Chateau in the
Loire Valley, and she is helping
to reunite us too.

I'm getting excited because they have finalized plans with Air Transport Services for a Sheep Air to safely transport my family to Dulles Airport in Virginia.

They have hired Barcode, the Border
Collie, to be their Guide Dog.
Once at Dulles Airport they will get a
transport truck and travel to
Gardiner's Grange.

Meanwhile, there was a lorry near
the entrance to Gardiner's Grange,
and I heard that it was going
into town.

I quickly got on the lorry and ended
up in town. While window shopping
I stopped at Sally's Shearing Salon.

I got a trim and a snack
and got back home.

Later, I went to the top of Blue Ridge
Mountain, and I saw lots of friends.
It was a beautiful day.
I talked to my friend, Rose.

There was one particular sheep
that came to talk to me.
I liked him and he liked me.
His name was Wooliam.

A month went by.
I was out in the field.
I heard a very, very large truck
coming up the road to
Gardiner's Grange.

I was so
excited.

VAROOM!

The truck was bringing my family.

When they arrived everyone
unpacked their bags and
planned to stay.

GARDINER'S GRANGE

I got so excited and jumped

around and around.

My family and all the children,
all the sheep, dogs, goats, and
cows celebrated.

There were lots of toys,
balloons and games.
Even our new dog friends,
Bryan and Bill,
celebrated with us.

Now I have my family and friends...

and I am so happy, happy, happy.